ACHIEVING
PRODUCTIVITY

ORGANIZE YOUR PHYSICAL AND DIGITAL WORKSPACE

Getting your physical and digital workspaces organized is a great way to be more productive. In this book, you'll learn the rewards of a more organized workspace. You'll find out what a productive workspace looks like and how to declutter your workspace to match.

You'll learn how to manage your digital workspace and how to tame the e-mail monster. And finally, you'll find out how to make your new clutter-free life last by making organization a habit.

GETTING MOTIVATED TO BECOME ORGANIZED

After completing this topic, you should be able to recognize the rewards of an organized workspace.

Do you have the kind of desk that your mother would be ashamed of? When you're looking for an important file, do you have to search through back issues of trade mags and old lunch menus? Does it take you much longer than it should to prepare for meetings because you can't quickly lay your hands on everything you need? Okay, maybe you're not quite this disorganized, but you probably know someone who is. Nearly everyone has dealt with workplace clutter at one time or another. If you have, you know that it can range from mildly annoying, to practically paralyzing.

Either way, clutter can have a serious, negative impact on productivity. The key to being productive is organization. When you work in an office, your workspace is central to everything you do. So keeping it organized is essential to being effective in your job. If you need a little motivation for changing your ways, let's explore the rewards of an organized workspace.

The first is that it projects professionalism. First impressions matter, and your workspace is often the first impression your colleagues and clients have of you. And even if your work is impeccable, a messy workspace sends a different message. Would you rather project an image of being organized or of being overwhelmed and unable to handle your workload? Another reward is that it decreases stress.

A disorganized workspace can make you feel you don't have your work under control, and this can increase your stress levels. *[A horizontal bar graph, representing stress levels, is displayed. There are three bars, titled "Very stressful," "Somewhat stressful," and "Not at all stressful" respectively. The longest bar is "Somewhat stressful" and the shortest bar is "Not at all stressful."]*

If you reduce the stress by getting organized, you can focus on excelling at your job, instead of worrying about it. *[The "Not at all stressful" bar is now the longest and the "Very stressful bar is now the shortest. The bar titled "Somewhat stressful" decreases in length.]* The third reward you reap by organizing your workspace is that it can improve your outlook. Your desk is the first thing you see when you arrive at work, and if you work in an office, you spend many hours there every day. That means that the state of your workspace can have a big influence on your daily outlook on life.

A disorganized space can make you feel frustrated, helpless, and annoyed. But a tidy, organized space can significantly boost your mood, and improve your state of mind. Finally, organizing your workspace can increase your long-term productivity. When you're able to find everything you need easily, you can spend your time being productive, not overwhelmed. Taking the time now to organize your workspace, and keep it organized, can help you become a more effective, focused employee.

DESIGNING A PRODUCTIVE WORKSPACE

After completing this topic, you should be able to recognize what a productive workspace looks like.

When you think of a typical workspace, you probably imagine a room or cubical, maybe with a few filing cabinets or shelves. There is likely a desk covered in papers with a computer on it. Maybe your own workspace looks like this, but unfortunately, this isn't what a productive workspace looks like. Effective workspace management means starting from the biggest areas, the filing system or shelves. Then you work your way down to the smallest, the digital filing system on your computer. The first step in designing a productive workspace is to create a minimalist workspace.

To do this, you should get rid of as many extra items in your space as possible. Extra items mean clutter, and clutter leads to distraction. So keep only the things that are necessary. Next, you need usable desk space. You can't use your desk if it's covered in paper and files. So clear it off to give yourself room to work. The third step is to make sure that everything you use regularly is within arm's reach.

This way, you'll avoid wasting time and causing interruptions by having to get out of your chair to retrieve things. Finally, it's easy to be productive when you have neatly organized shelves and filing systems. It might be good to set up clearly labeled, color-coded hanging folders, or to put a small file box on your desk for frequently used items. It's also useful to organize books in alphabetical order and use bins to organize smaller items.

Let's consider an example. Jorge is an accountant at a prestigious accounting firm. He's hoping for a promotion, and his boss has hinted that his messy office doesn't put across the image of a competent accountant. So Jorge has decided to get organized. First, he gets rid of everything he doesn't need. He tosses old memos, take-out menus, and newsletters, anything he doesn't need to do his job.

Next, Jorge gets to work on his desk. He clears everything off, and the only things that go back on are his computer, a small desktop filing system, and a printer. Jorge has a large filing cabinet in his office, as well as a small bookshelf. Although he can usually locate files, he knows his current system doesn't really make sense. So he reorganizes his files alphabetically by client name. This makes it easier for him and his assistants to retrieve files quickly.

He takes all the books off his bookshelf, and replaces only the reference books he uses regularly. When Jorge is finished, he's pretty happy with the results. But when he goes to grab a book, he realizes his bookshelf isn't within reach of his desk. So he moves the bookshelf nearer to his desk so everything is close at hand. If your workspace is more productive, then you will be too.

THE STEPS TO BECOMING CLUTTER-FREE

After completing this topic, you should be able to apply the process for creating a clutter-free workspace in a given scenario.

A clutter-free workspace can help increase your productivity. And there are three steps you can take to better manage your physical workspace. In the first step, you should visualize what you want to achieve and set goals. Picture your ideal workspace. What do you need in it to be productive? Where will you keep your current work? What kind of filing system would be best? Set goals to help achieve your vision. For example, one goal might be to stop missing deadlines because you're disorganized. Let's see how Bart handles this.

He's a project manager who has decided to clear out the clutter. He visualizes a clutter free, neatly organized office. His goals are to clear off his desk every day and to have a single location for all his project files. The second step is to organize one area at a time. Starting with a small area helps you stay motivated, because you'll get immediate results without becoming overwhelmed. Going back to Bart, he starts with his desk. He clears off piles of paper, coffee cups, and old brochures. Then he puts only his laptop and phone back on the desk.

Finally, go through clutter and address paper overload. Take home non-work related belongings. When you sort through your paper clutter, be ruthless. If you can't think of a good reason to keep a piece of paper, discard it. If you throw away something you later need, you'll likely be able to get another copy. If you find a piece of paper that someone else should take care of, pass it along. Delegating tasks is one key to personal productivity.

You may find a piece of paper that you might need in the future. If so, you can file it away. But before you file something, ask yourself what would happen if you couldn't find it again? If the answer is nothing, discard it. Some pieces of paper require you to take action, such as letters that need a response. You can create a file labeled action for these. So when our friend Bart is de-cluttering his paper, he finds an old sales report that he thinks he might need someday, but he decides to discard it.

His company keeps a digital copy of reports. So if he ever needs the information, he can look there. Bart finds a list of sales leads, which he passes along to the head of sales. He also finds a large pile of business cards, these might be useful in the future, so he creates a file for business contacts. When he finds a proposal that he needs to read, he places it in his action file so he'll remember to do it soon. When the clutter is gone, you'll find it was worth the effort, as you settle into work in your neatly organized workspace.

SETTING UP AN EFFECTIVE PAPER FILING SYSTEM

After completing this topic, you should be able to recognize appropriate examples of the principles of effective filing.

Developing an effective filing system helps you find things when they're needed. Then you can avoid wasting time looking for things and instead you can get right to work. Three steps can help you to create an effective filing system. The first step in creating your system is to sort like with like and consolidate files into basic general categories. You could begin by sorting paper into groups on your desk and identifying the patterns that emerge. For instance, suppose you noticed three general categories.

Your company's five-year plan, your department's five-year plan, and a copy of your company's annual goals. These could all be consolidated into one file, labeled with your company's name, and the heading, Planning. Don't get fancy with file labeling. That's the second step in good file management. Label your files using common sense, not elaborate, imaginative titles. You could choose to file them alphabetically.

But there are lots of other ways to categorize files. You could sort by subject, numerically, geographically or chronologically, whichever makes most sense to you and to the subject matter you're dealing with. It's also useful to label files with nouns. For example, a label titled Contract Negotiations makes more sense than How to Negotiate Contracts?

It's a good idea to label files according to how you use information rather than where you found it. For instance, maybe you regularly save articles from newsletters or magazines. It will be easier to find these later if you file them according to the subject of the article rather than the name of the source. *[For example, articles about finance could be stored in a folder titled "Finance Articles".]*

The third step is to purge files regularly, by getting rid of information you no longer need. Purging files helps you maintain a clutter-free filing system because you only keep things that are truly needed. You should try to turn every piece of paper in your workspace into an action item. Deal with each piece before it has the chance to become clutter.

For example, say you come back from a conference with a pile of business cards. It's best to either deal with them immediately by filing or discarding or else put them into an action folder to deal with soon.

The same principle applies to every piece of paper you encounter. If you can't action it immediately, figure out how to deal with it before it ends up in a pile on your desk. If you follow the principles of effective filing, you'll find that your time can be spent on your work instead of on dealing with chaos.

MANAGING DIGITAL FILES

After completing this topic, you should be able to recognize techniques for managing digital files.

Your computer is a key part of your work space, so you need to keep it in order. A cluttered computer can lower your productivity just as much as a cluttered office can. So it's important to manage your digital files well. You can increase your productivity by practicing good digital file-management techniques. First, you need a good filing system. You wouldn't dump files randomly into a filing cabinet and you shouldn't do it with your computer files either.

The best way to organize digital files is to think of your computer as an electronic filing cabinet, and mirror your paper filing system. Just as you would with the file cabinet, you should set up general categories, group applications and files, and sub-categorize. This will make it easier to quickly find what you're looking for. You can organize your files in the way that makes most sense for you. For instance, your file categories could include Projects, Customers, Content, or Date. For the next technique, when you're setting up your digital filing system, use consistent, logical naming to make it easier to find files later.

Use nouns for names. For instance, Archives, Invoices, and Taxes. Use file names that make most sense to you, but remember, a file's title should make it absolutely clear what it contains. For instance, if you have a lot of documents relating to your vehicle, such as warranty and finance information, a logical file name would be simply Car. The third technique is to use versioning, to keep track of documents and ensure you can always find the most recent version.

The file name should make the version of a document clear. Say you're updating a file named Property Management Report. You could name the new copy, Property Management Report Version 2, so that the most recent document is easy to find. Finally, make sure your computer's desktop doesn't look like an electronic to-do list. It shouldn't be where you keep every single document you're currently working on. Instead, apply the final technique.

Organize your desktop system to make filing and categorizing easy. For instance, you could start by creating three folders, Working, Reference, and Archive. Then you could organize files in these folders according to their importance right at this moment. You should back up all files before you begin deleting folders and reorganizing documents, whether to an external hard drive, cloud storage, or server. When you can find everything you need on your computer, you'll find your working day is much less stressful.

STAYING ON TOP
OF E-MAIL

After completing this topic, you should be able to manage your e-mail in a given scenario.

The number of e-mails you receive can be overwhelming. But if you stay on top of your e-mail, your productivity will increase. You'll keep up with everything you need to know because you won't miss important e-mails among the clutter. To better manage your e-mail, let's explore three techniques. First, you should manage your inbox methodically and regularly. If you carry out routine management, you won't get overwhelmed. A good way is to regularly delete unwanted e-mails.

Make a decision as you read each e-mail and delete it if it has no value. The second technique to stay on top of your e-mail is to file or archive e-mails you want to keep. Don't leave everything in your inbox, set up folders within your e-mail system so they mirror your paper filing system. Then transfer the e- mails you want to keep into the appropriate folders.

Use logical folder names so you can easily find e- mails. And get in the habit of moving e-mails to the correct folder as soon as you've read them. Spam messages can take up a lot of your time if you don't manage them. So it's important to take control of spam, the third technique for managing e-mail effectively. One of the best ways is to use an effective Internet service provider, or ISP, to block spam. It's also worthwhile investing in a powerful spam blocker. And don't forget to set the security on your e-mail to its highest level.

Let's explore an example. Travis is a senior executive who gets more than 100 e-mails a day. His inbox contains more than 400 messages. He's finding it more and more difficult to keep track of what is important, so he needs to take control of his e-mail. The first thing he does is open every message.

He makes an immediate decision on each one, and deletes any message that contains information he doesn't need, or, that he could easily find elsewhere. Next, Travis sets up an e-mail filing system. He creates one folder for e-mails that require action. Another folder is for reference e-mails that contain useful information, but don't need immediate action.

And a third folder is for permanent e-mails that he won't need to refer to very often. Finally, Travis deals with spam. He knows he's let his anti-spam software expire, so he renews his subscription. He also does some research and switches to an ISP that has a good track record on blocking spam. When you don't see that big number in the unread column of your inbox, you'll feel less stressed, and you can be more productive.

MAKING ORGANIZATION A HABIT

After completing this topic, you should be able to recognize how to maintain a productive workspace.

Getting organized will benefit you in many ways. You'll probably be more productive and you'll feel more confident. But getting organized is only half the battle. If you want to keep enjoying all those benefits, you have to make organization a habit. Four behavior changes can help you make an organized workspace become a habit. First, you need to handle each item as it comes in.

If you aren't careful, stacks of paper can quickly pile up. To avoid that, take immediate action on each piece of paper and every digital file as you receive it. Let's use Kathy, an executive assistant, as an example. She keeps all her papers in a filing cabinet so they don't pile up on her desk. Every time something comes across her desk it gets filed that same day. So that brings us to the second behavior change – keep paper and digital filing systems up to date.

Returning to Kathy, she regularly goes through her paper and digital files. She consolidates categories that overlap, and she creates new categories when they're needed. And she checks regularly to make sure everything that she's kept is useful and discards whatever is no longer needed. You should deal with your files daily, weekly, and monthly. If you have an action folder of work, go through it often and determine if any of the items can be filed away.

Every day Kathy files all the papers on her desk. Each week she transfers projects she's completed into the archive area of her filing cabinet. Finally, at the end of the month, she goes through her filing cabinet and gets rid of any files she no longer needs. The third behavior change is forming a habit of clearing your desk every night. If a messy desk is the first thing you see when you go into your office, it's difficult to be productive for the rest of the day.

A clean desk means a clean slate. So if Kathy is in the middle of something when the day ends, she files it away appropriately. And the final behavior change for maintaining an organized workspace is to add notes where they belong, not on random pieces of paper. Suppose a client calls our friend Kathy and that client wants to update her contact information. Instead of jotting it down on a sticky note, Kathy takes out the client's file and adds the information where it belongs.

This technique can save you countless minutes in a day. If you jot notes on random pieces of paper, you have to rewrite the information where it belongs. So you're doing the same work twice. Making organization a habit doesn't take very long. It's just a matter of repeating the same actions until they become second nature. You might even be the envy of your organizationally challenged colleagues.

AVOID PROCRASTINATION BY GETTING ORGANIZED INSTEAD

Procrastination makes you a less effective employee, and causes you stress at the same time. In this book, you'll learn about the reasons people procrastinate, *[Fear of giving up control, lack of self-discipline, being overwhelmed, lack of interest, and fear of failing are some of the reasons behind procrastination.]* and the rewards you'll reap when you overcome procrastination.

You'll learn how to build self-discipline and fight time wasters. And finally, you'll find out how to set priorities and focus on achieving them, and how to say no when you need to.

1. The Benefits of Overcoming Procrastination
2. Why People Procrastinate
3. Developing Self-discipline
4. Combating Time Wasters
5. Keeping Priorities in Focus
6. Learning How to Say "No"

THE BENEFITS
OF OVERCOMING
PROCRASTINATION

After completing this topic, you should be able to recognize the benefits of overcoming procrastination.

Do you ever put off doing tasks that you really should do right away? Do you find yourself playing solitaire when you should be writing a report? Or chatting at the water cooler instead of getting down to business on those first quarter results? If you do, you're not alone. This bad habit is called procrastination. Say you're a financial analyst for an insurance company.

And you're supposed to fact- check the organization's financial results before they're published in two days' time. You know that to get it done right, you'll need to work on it most of today and tomorrow. But you're a serial procrastinator. So you convince yourself that it would be better to start tomorrow morning when you're fresh, and you relax by going for coffee with a coworker. You likely already know that your behavior will have consequences. The results won't be ready on time and you may find yourself in deep trouble because of it. That's the most obvious consequence.

When you waste time, things don't get done when they should. But there are other consequences, too. You're probably often stressed and anxious, and your colleagues probably get frustrated with you. And the constant delays in your output cause problems for your company, too. On the other hand, if you can manage to overcome that bad habit of procrastinating, you'll find that you'll reap several rewards from doing so. This week, you've been assigned the task of assessing investment opportunities for your organization. And you've decided that you're going to beat procrastination. So you make a plan and you avoid getting distracted.

And for once, you deliver a project on time. That decision to keep your plan shows the first reward of overcoming procrastination. It helps you achieve more. Over the next two weeks, you get your day-to-day tasks done quicker. And now that you're not always in a rush at the last minute, the quality of your work improves. *[A bar graph, representing improvement in SKILLS over a period of time, is displayed.]* This shows the second reward of overcoming procrastination.

People who don't procrastinate do better professionally. Remember when you didn't check those financial results? Well, that caused a company-wide emergency.
The press didn't get the results when they were meant to, and stocks fell. But now that you've changed your ways, you can avoid crisis in the future. The third reward of overcoming procrastination. Within a few months, your stress levels drop.

Before, when you were still a procrastinator, you used to spend weekends worrying about looming deadlines, because you knew you hadn't done what was necessary to meet them. Now you can take that time for yourself. That's the fourth reward. When you overcome procrastination, you have more time for yourself and to relax. Getting more done, doing better in your career, staying out of crisis, and having more time. All those rewards of overcoming procrastination sound good, don't they? So what are you waiting for?

WHY PEOPLE PROCRASTINATE

After completing this topic, you should be able to recognize the causes of workplace procrastination.

If you're the kind of person who puts off everything until the last minute, you probably already know that your procrastination is holding you back from achieving your potential. *[Two horizontal bars, titled Potential and Achieved, are displayed, which indicate that your achievement will be less compared to your potential when you procrastinate.]* But do you know why you procrastinate in the first place? Many people don't know the underlying cause for this kind of behavior. But if you understand why something happens, it makes it that much easier to change it. There are some common causes of procrastination at work. Let's explore them and how they might crop up in the workplace.

The first is fear of failing, which often comes about because you have unrealistic expectations of yourself. Let's say you're part of the sales department at a publishing company, and your boss asks you to research national buying patterns for e-books. You don't have much experience in doing research, and you're afraid that what you come up with won't be up to par.

So you avoid getting started on the project for as long as you can. And eventually you write a rushed paper that disappoints your boss. Your fear of failing caused you to fail. The next cause is fear of giving up control. Procrastinators often don't like deadlines, because they think that deadlines take away their own control over their work. For example, a financial planner is writing a department budget plan, which is supposed to be discussed at a meeting before it's incorporated into the organization's overall budget. But the financial planner procrastinates so that his proposal won't be ready until after the meeting.

He thinks that if the plan isn't ready in time, it won't be challenged. But instead, he just looks unreliable. The third common cause of procrastination is a lack of interest in the task at hand. Sometimes you just want to avoid a boring task.

For instance, an employee in an HR department has been asked to reorganize five years of employee complaint files, categorizing each one according to the method of complaint. But the employee thinks the task is beneath her, and besides, it's time consuming and dull. So, she avoids doing it. And as a result, the task isn't done in time for an important employment strategy launch. Just because a task is boring to you doesn't make it unimportant.

The final common cause is being overwhelmed. When you're overwhelmed, sometimes you don't know where to begin a task, and so you delay starting it. For example, imagine you're a PR exec with a telecom company, and you've been put in charge of a nationwide competition for customers.

But you've never organized anything that involved so many different tasks. So you get overwhelmed. As a result, you avoid starting the project, which, of book, means you're already behind schedule. Getting a handle on why you're delaying can help you stop procrastinating, and start getting things done.

DEVELOPING SELF-DISCIPLINE

After completing this topic, you should be able to recognize ways to develop discipline in a given scenario.

One problem that many procrastinators share is that they don't have self-discipline. Luckily, there are some ways you can develop it. First, work during your best times. Chart your energy levels over a day's work. Divide your day into two hour segments and note whether your energy levels are high, moderate, or low. Repeat this across the week to give you a picture of your average working day.

[Sample vertical bars, representing Energy levels, are displayed for four time slots for Monday to Friday – 9:00 a.m. to 11:00 a.m., 11:00 a.m. to 1:00 p.m., 1:00 p.m. to 3:00 p.m., and 3:00 p.m. to 5:00 p.m. The vertical bar for the 9:00 a.m. to 11:00 a.m. time slot is titled High. The vertical bar for the 11:00 a.m. to 1:00 p.m. time slot is titled Moderate, and it is roughly half the length of the vertical bar titled High.

The vertical bar for the 1:00 p.m. to 3:00 p.m. time slot is titled Low, and it is roughly half the length of the vertical bar titled Moderate. The vertical bar for the 3:00 p.m. to 5:00 p.m. time slot is also titled Moderate.] Then schedule your most important work for your best hours, when you're most energetic. Let's work through an example. An IT consultant who's prone to procrastination has decided to change her ways.

She analyses her energy levels and finds that she works best between 11:00 a.m. and 1:00 p.m. *[Sample vertical bars, representing*

Energy levels, are displayed for four time slots – 9:00 a.m. to 11:00 a.m. time slot titled Moderate, 11:00 a.m. to 1:00 p.m. time slot titled High, 1:00 p.m. to 3:00 p.m. time slot titled Moderate, and 3:00 p.m. to 5:00 p.m. time slot titled Low. The vertical bar for the 11 a.m. to 1:00 p.m. time slot is highlighted.] So she schedules her most difficult tasks for that time.

The next way to develop discipline is to stop thinking and just get started. Planning is important, but eventually you have to get the work done, otherwise you're just using the planning process to avoid the job. So that IT consultant is managing a network infrastructure changeover for a client.

She's made a plan, but instead of getting going, she asks some contacts for ideas and spends a week weighing the pros and cons of their opinions. In the end, she sticks with her original plan, so that week was time wasted. That moves us onto the third way to be more self-disciplined. Make neatness a habit. Invest some time in neatness and you'll soon save time by not having to search for things. Keep your desk and computer tidy. Create digital and paper filing systems and keep them up to date.

Our IT consultant friend has a tidy computer already, but her desk is a mess. She makes time one afternoon to get things cleaned up. And from then on, she can quickly lay her hands on everything she needs. The final strategy for self-discipline is to focus on finishing.

Don't get bogged down in perfectionism. It's good to want the work to be excellent, but you have to be able to let go of a task, too. Also, don't get distracted by new tasks. Get your current work done before you start something else. It can help to reward yourself to keep motivated, so you could promise yourself a break after you've reached a target.

Our IT consultant's making a plan for a company system upgrade. She works solidly, rewarding herself with a decaf mocha every time she finishes three sections. Another client calls for a consult, but she schedules a future call for when she's finished, and she keeps going until the job is done instead of second guessing herself and adding bells and whistles. If you want to get things done, when you feel like giving up, you need to act on what you think instead of what you feel. Build self-discipline and that's what you'll be able to do.

COMBATING TIME WASTERS

After completing this topic, you should be able to match the actions to take to combat time wasters.

You're in the middle of a big project, and you need to get back to work. But how about quickly checking your e-mail first? Or maybe a quick look at your social networking site to see how everyone's doing? Avoiding time wasters like this is vital to developing self-discipline.

The time and energy you waste isn't just the minutes you're on the phone or the Internet. You waste more time when you get back to work, because you have to review what you've already done. You can use strategies to help you avoid the most common time wasters. The first time waster is e-mail and the Internet. To avoid endless hours reading mails, set up separate e-mail accounts for work and personal use. Stop continuously checking your e-mail. Do it only at regular intervals. File your e-mail in appropriate folders.

As for the Internet, think of a task you could be doing instead of surfing and close that browser. The second time waster is telephone calls. Tell your friends and family only to call in emergencies. When you're busy at work, tell your co-workers only to call if it's urgent. Speaking of your co-workers, that's the third time waster, interruptions from colleagues.

Let them know when you're available to talk and when you're not. If you have to, find a new space to work in, whether it's at home or somewhere else in your office. If you have an office with a door, close it. And you can suggest that your company establishes a designated quiet time when employees can work without interruption. The fourth time waster is personal reading material.

The best way to deal with this one is to get rid of it. Clear your workspace completely of newspapers or magazines that don't concern your work. And, finally, the bane of many office workers, unnecessary meetings. Make sure the meetings you attend have a clear agenda. Don't let meetings run longer than scheduled. And make sure you assign action items, so you don't find yourself in another meeting about the same thing with no progress made.

You should identify your personal time wasters that cause trouble in your work day and come up with ways to deal with them. For example, for you, it might be the 30 minute break that turns into a 45 minute one, or the unnecessary and energy sapping meetings. Maybe the problem is that your lunch break usually runs long because you eat at your computer, and lose yourself in reading the news online. So you might decide to eat lunch in the cafeteria instead.

As for the meetings, you might decide to have a chat with your boss and explain that they're becoming unmanageable. Your boss might be fine with you skipping any meetings that don't relate to your workload. When you eliminate your own time wasters, you'll find you can get a whole lot more done.

KEEPING PRIORITIES IN FOCUS

After completing this topic, you should be able to recognize how to set priorities and keep focused.

Have you ever found yourself torn between one task and another, dropping one thing to do something else, and then finding you're behind with both? You can avoid this kind of thing if you take steps to set priorities and keep focused. Your first action is to clearly define your goals. Goals help you avoid getting distracted, and they make you concentrate on your destination. It's best to make your goals measurable and specific.

Next, prioritize your activities. Look at all the tasks in front of you, and decide which is most important. It's good to split them into low-priority, medium-priority, and high-priority tasks. Deal with them in order of importance. Then you want to break projects down into elements that you can complete one at a time. Finally, if you want to keep focused in the long term, you should become a planner.

You might think that's just not you. Well, in fact, anyone can learn to plan, by developing a few habits. *[A two-column table is displayed with the headings Task and Time required. The first column contains the task names. The second column contains the number of hours required to complete the respective task.]* First, plan continuously. As you move through a plan, add to it all the time.

Analyze how things are going as you work, and change or alter your plan when you need to. *[A task log sheet, which contains the reports for each of the working days in a week and the progress made during the week, is displayed.]* Second, start your day early. Think about how you plan to achieve your goals, and create an action plan for the day. And finally, when you finish your work day, start planning the next. While the things you need to do are fresh in your mind, write them down, so you'll have something to build on tomorrow. Let's explore an example. A PR exec has a busy month ahead.

She defines her goals for the month, she has to work on a marketing strategy for a new product, arrange radio interviews for her company's CEO, and meet with a TV ad agency about a new campaign. Next, she prioritizes her activities. The marketing strategy is very important, so she needs to get on that right away.

She can talk to the TV ad agency when she gets a chance. And she delegates the radio interviews to a junior colleague. The marketing strategy is a big project, so she breaks it down. First, she needs to meet with the product development department about it. That's number one. After that, she can brainstorm ideas with her team. Then, she needs to get buy-in from the CEO. Finally, the PR exec starts to become a planner.

She adds targets to her marketing strategy as she goes along. For example, after the product development department meeting, she realizes she needs to talk to another team about a related product. She puts that on her end-of-day list, and in the morning, she makes an action item to arrange that meeting. Setting priorities, and keeping focused on them, is key to an effective and directed work life. *[High priority, medium priority, and low priority are grouped under the heading "Prioritize your activities."]*

LEARNING HOW TO SAY "NO"

After completing this topic, you should be able to identify ways to say "no" and avoid overcommitment.

It's easy to get overcommitted when you don't know how to say no to anything. You might be afraid that people will be annoyed if you say no. But imagine how annoyed they'll be after you say yes and can't do what you've agreed to. There are four steps you can take to help you learn to say no. First off, give yourself permission to say no. You have to value your own time.

Don't feel guilty for not giving it up, you're not letting anyone down. Remind yourself why it is that you have to turn down the request. So if you're feeling guilty because your line manager asked you to create a new action plan, and you had to say no because you're working on an urgent troubleshooting problem for the CTO, remind yourself that your current task is crucial.

The second step is to be realistic about the consequences of any commitment. Look at the tasks already on your plate before you take on something else, and don't get side-tracked away from your existing commitments. Don't feel you have to answer every request on the spot. You can always say you'll answer later. For instance, you've been asked for a research report that will take roughly 50 hours and needs to be done in three weeks. You review your workload and find you can only free up 30 hours in the next three weeks. So you get back to your boss and say no. That's being realistic about making commitments.

The third step in saying no is to be direct and assertive. This doesn't mean being rude. Be firm, but be polite. And it helps to explain your reasons for saying no. Like explaining firmly that you can't fix bugs in company software until the system upgrade is finished. Otherwise, nobody will be able to use the system at all.

Believe me, your boss will completely understand. The fourth step is to offer alternatives and solutions. Suppose your manager asks you to do something, but you're already swamped. You could suggest that one of your current tasks be postponed or delegated to someone else. Let's say, you've been asked to train employees on new company methods, but you're already working on inducting a group of interns.

First you say no to the new task, but your boss says it's a priority. So you suggest a junior colleague could take over with the interns, and your boss agrees. Learning to say no and then sticking with it is a big part of prioritizing better and overcoming procrastination. If you're clear about your priorities and you say no to anything that keeps you from achieving your goals, you'll find you're more productive and on the road to professional success. *[A bar graph, representing improvement in SKILLS over a period of time, is displayed.]*

MAXIMIZE YOUR PRODUCTIVITY BY MANAGING TIME AND TASKS

While your time is limited, it's possible to do more with your time by being more productive – producing more value in the time you have. In this book, you'll learn about managing tasks in a way that maximizes your productivity.

You'll discover the benefits of assessing the time and value of your tasks, identifying your priorities, chunking your time, building a schedule, creating an effective to-do list, and making effective use of your to-do list.

1. Assessing the Time and Value of Your Tasks

2. Prioritizing Tasks to Pinpoint Your Priorities

3. Chunking Your Time

4. Building a Schedule

5. Creating an Effective To-do List

6. Making Effective Use of a To-do List

ASSESSING THE TIME AND VALUE OF YOUR TASKS

After completing this topic, you should be able to sequence the steps for assessing the time and value of your tasks.

Successful businesspeople recognize that time has value. And they recognize too that it needs to be managed like any valuable asset. That's why it's important to use your time as productively as possible. To ensure you're using your time productively, you need to assess the time and value of your tasks. There are some steps you can follow to assess the time and value of your tasks.

The first step is to identify your goals.
You improve productivity by taking control of whatever's obstructing your efforts to achieve your goals. The Pareto principle - also known as the 80/20 rule, which basically says that 80% of effects come from 20% of causes - is a good start.

This suggests that 80% of the results achieved come from 20% of the tasks performed. So doesn't it make sense to identify the most valuable tasks and give them more time?
The second step is to log the time spent on tasks, so you have an accurate picture of how you spend your time. A task log records the precise amount of time you spend on various tasks each day, with columns for the task, time started, and minutes used. Additional columns categorize the tasks.

As soon as you do something, log it. And always include personal tasks like calling home, distractions like browsing online, and small tasks like traveling to an internal meeting.

The third step is to find the patterns in your time use. Do this by gathering and analyzing your task logs for one week. With this data, you'll be able to identify how you spend your time - and when you're most productive.

Since you've categorized your tasks in the logs, it'll be easy to pinpoint imbalances in the types of tasks taking up your time. For example, are you spending too much time doing paperwork, helping out colleagues, or socializing at work? Maybe there are times of day when you're regularly interrupted. Your logs can tell you. Highlighting "time wasters" show where there's scope to improve productivity.

The fourth step is to identify the tasks that produce the most value. Highest value tasks are those that are both aligned to your goals and have a high potential to impact the success of your work.

Ask yourself, "How does this task contribute toward achieving my goals?" Tasks that move you in the right strategic direction are more important than those that don't.

Also consider tasks in terms of consequences – the potential impact of the task. So ask yourself, "What are the possible consequences of not doing this task?"

Your time is too valuable to waste. And you need to use it as productively as possible. Maximizing productivity begins with assessing the time and value of your tasks. And by following these simple steps, you'll be well on your way.

PRIORITIZING TASKS TO PINPOINT YOUR PRIORITIES

After completing this topic, you should be able to match the types of tasks that belong in four priority categories.

Whenever you're busy and tasks are piling up in front of you, it can be hard sometimes to see the forest for the trees. Every task is screaming out for attention. But not all tasks are created equally. That's why it's important to identify your priorities. Priorities are the tasks and activities that take precedence over others.

One way to prioritize tasks and activities is to use a priority matrix. *[The Priority Matrix has columns for Time Sensitive and Not time sensitive tasks, and rows for High value and Low value tasks. It contains four quadrants, one for each combination of time sensitivity and value.]* This classifies tasks in terms of how valuable and time sensitive they are. It's a simple tool that lets you categorize tasks or activities as critical, high, medium, or low priority. Let's look at each of these.

Tasks that are time sensitive and high value are critical priorities. These include crises and deadlines. Tasks that are high value, but not time sensitive, are high priorities. These are tasks that involve thinking, planning, and collaboration. Although they fall into your longer-term plans, they should be started as soon as possible. Otherwise, they'll become time sensitive.

Tasks that are time sensitive, but not high value, are medium priorities. Medium priorities include some meetings and some correspondence. Tasks that are neither time sensitive nor high value are low priorities. These can be postponed, dropped, or delegated. They include time wasters and doing favors.

A priority matrix is a good way to prioritize the activities in your daily task logs. Just consider where each task would fit in terms of the matrix. Make a list and assign priorities. Use 1 for critical tasks – time sensitive and high value. Use 2 for high – high value but not time sensitive. Use 3 for medium – time sensitive but low value. And use 4 for low – neither time sensitive nor high value.

Let's explore how an editorial manager at a publishing company figured out the value of her tasks. She's logged her tasks daily for a week, and now she's ready to prioritize her tasks and determine how she's spending her time.

She notes her morning was spent checking edits on a final manuscript, but notices a pattern of interruptions – mostly from colleagues. She then analyzes her tasks in terms of goals and consequences. This gives her the high-value tasks. She then determines which tasks are time sensitive. Finally, she uses a priority matrix to assign a priority to each task.

The tasks that are high value and time sensitive are categorized as critical priority. Those that are high value but not time sensitive are categorized as high priority. Whatever is time sensitive but low value gets categorized as medium priority. And anything that's neither high value nor time sensitive is categorized as low priority.

When you're up against it, everything seems urgent - and that can be overwhelming. But not everything on your to-do list is a priority. And that's why it's important to know how to identify priorities - and to tell the difference between a critical priority at one extreme and a low priority at the other.

CHUNKING YOUR TIME

After completing this topic, you should be able to recognize how to chunk your time.

Do you ever wish there were more hours in the day? Many people do. They think that having more time means doing more. But personal productivity isn't about putting in more hours on the job. It's about optimizing your work schedule by planning, organizing, and controlling your use of time more effectively. The answer to making the most of your time is "chunking." Chunking is an organizational strategy for making more efficient use of your time schedule. It means arranging your schedule, so you have segments of time dedicated to one task or type of activity.

Chunking time can boost productivity because focusing on one thing at a time saves the time wasted on task switching. And it can improve your state of mind, letting you concentrate on completing a task in full. And you can give yourself a 'job done' pat on the back!

Chunking needs to be done as you're creating your work schedule. Consider what you need to accomplish. If you've kept task logs during the week, you'll have a good idea of what you do during a typical week. And then follow three simple guidelines.

Each time you shift your attention from one thing to another, you lose focus. And reorienting yourself to the task at hand takes up time. So the first guideline is to group similar tasks and activities together into the same chunk of time. This will cut time loss. For example, you could cluster together your written correspondence – your e-mail, letters, memos, reports – and schedule a chunk of time for all that.

Or if you have regular meetings outside the office, you could schedule them together and save time on travel. The second guideline is to insert chunks of time into your written schedule. Treat these chunks of time with respect and insert them into your schedule just as you would any other priority item, like a meeting. When chunks are included in your schedule, they're part of your routine. For example, you could schedule a chunk of time each morning for making personal contact with clients or colleagues.

The final guideline is allow at least an hour of uninterrupted time for each chunk in your schedule. This stops you wasting time task switching. Minimize interruptions by explaining to colleagues that you're not available to them during these times. Unless it's necessary for the task at hand, don't check your e-mail or answer the phone. You can reply to messages later. If you're polite and consistent, people will come to accept this time as part of your work routine.

Some people believe multitasking is the way to get more out of their time. In fact, that couldn't be further from the truth. Multitasking actually wastes time. Instead of doing lots of different tasks at the same time, you should dedicate yourself to one task. That's chunking. And that's the silver bullet.

BUILDING A SCHEDULE

After completing this topic, you should be able to recognize the basic principles of scheduling.

A big part of management is organization. And a big part of organization is scheduling. So if you want to better manage your team, it's a good idea to create a written schedule. A schedule is important for personal productivity because it gives a holistic view of what has to be done during a particular period of time.

It also helps you organize your time wisely, allowing enough time to complete important tasks, and keeping time to deal with surprises. There are seven basic principles involved in personal scheduling. The first principle is to compile the schedule just prior to the period of time covered. This helps keep it relevant and cuts out the need for multiple revisions. The time covered in your schedule should be dependent on the tasks and their deadlines.

The next principle is to begin your schedule with the end in mind. This means starting with the objectives you have to achieve. Decide what has to be finished by the end of each day or week. These are your "deliverables" – time-sensitive tasks that must be completed by a deadline.

Principle number three is to schedule critical-priority tasks first. Critical tasks are high-value – important to achieving your goals – and time-sensitive tasks. After critical-priority tasks have been scheduled, look to high-priority tasks, then medium-priority tasks, and then – if there's time left – low-priority tasks.

The next principle of scheduling is to recognize your controllable time. Having figured out what you need to accomplish, figure out how much time you actually have to achieve those objectives. It's unrealistic to schedule a full eight hours of vital tasks in every workday. What's you controllable time?

That's the actual time you have available to complete your scheduled tasks. You can calculate it by deducting the time you typically spend dealing with unpredictable events – these include routine interruptions, like requests from your boss or ad hoc conversations with colleagues, and situations or crises that have to be addressed –from the number of hours in your workday.

The fifth principle of scheduling is to allow time for previously unfinished critical tasks. Sometimes during the book of your day, you'll have to deal with issues that are both out of your control and unexpected. So no matter how efficiently you plan, you may not always have time to complete critical tasks within your schedule. You'll need "catch-up" time to get back on track.

The next principle of scheduling is to chunk similar tasks and activities together. Chunking helps efficiency because it reduces time used task switching. And the final principle of scheduling is to be flexible in your approach. Don't be afraid to adjust and readjust your schedule as required. Think of your schedule as a living document that will evolve through updates and revisions during its lifetime.

These principles will help you create an effective personal schedule. And an effective personal schedule is a key building block of better personal productivity.

CREATING AN
EFFECTIVE TO-DO LIST

After completing this topic, you should be able to recognize what an effective to-do list looks like.

No matter how big your workload, it's a lot less daunting when you know exactly what you have to do and exactly when you have to do it. And you can get that information from the simplest of tools: a to-do list. A to-do list is a simple scheduling tool that captures all the important tasks you need to complete. They usually cover a day, but can cover a week, a month, or any other time period.

Crossing off the tasks on your to-do list can be a great motivator– who doesn't enjoy doing that– and a great way to monitor productivity.

Things on your to-do list could include meetings you're scheduled to attend, phone calls you have to make, e-mails you need to write, and decisions you have to make.

Although daily to-do lists are most common, they're not the only sort. Types of to-do lists include a daily to-do list, which is a list of action items to be completed within a business day.

Or you could have a projects to-do list, which itemizes the actions needed to meet deadlines and milestones for a specific project or initiative. *[For example, Phase 1 January, Phase 2 February, Phase 3 March, Phase 4 April, Phase 5 May.]* A long-term to-do list itemizes the tasks that are valuable for working toward your goals, but aren't time sensitive. These may be tasks you want to do at some point, but don't have the time or resources to pursue at the present time.

An effective to-do list has three basic characteristics. First, It should be written down – it doesn't matter whether it's on paper or in electronic format. It's almost impossible to keep an accurate to-do list in your memory. Writing down your list and crossing off items will make sure it's accurate and up-to-date.

Next, it should be short – preferably ten items or fewer. Trying to add too many tasks could overwhelm you and set you up for failure. Think of your to-do list as a "top ten" list with the ten most valuable things you have to get done.

And, finally, the tasks should be prioritized by importance. The main purpose of a to-do list isn't to get everything done. It's to make sure that your most important tasks are completed. That's why to-do lists are prioritized. Prioritizing your list identifies which are the most important items in your schedule, and which can be postponed if necessary.

People use different designations and different levels of assessment for prioritizing tasks. Some classify tasks simply as urgent or not urgent. Others use A, B, C, D, or 1, 2, 3, or colors. It doesn't matter - all that matters is that the most critical tasks go at the top of the list.

A to-do list is one of the simplest scheduling tools imaginable, but don't be fooled: it's one of the best tools for guiding and monitoring your productivity.

MAKING EFFECTIVE USE OF A TO-DO LIST

After completing this topic, you should be able to analyze the use of a to-do list in a given scenario.

Creating a good to-do list counts for little if you don't use it effectively. Fortunately, there are guidelines that can help you use to-do lists more effectively. The first guideline is to break items down into achievable tasks. *[For example, divide Check e-mails into checking e-mails and answering e-mails.]* Complicated, loosely defined, or time-consuming activities should be broken down into smaller, achievable tasks.

The next is to create realistic objectives and time lines. Don't have too many items or items that simply aren't achievable. Time lines are also important. So consider how much time a task will need – and ensure you've scheduled enough.

The third guideline is to assign priorities to your list items. An effective to-do list prioritizes tasks in order of importance. You don't have to do the tasks in order, but prioritizing reminds you of your most critical tasks whenever you check the list.

Another guideline is to revise the list as needed. To be effective, the to-do list must be current. So review and amend your list regularly. Be ready to make changes based on completed tasks, revised deadlines, and unpredictable events.

The final guideline is to keep motivated. Efficiency and effectiveness have as much to do with motivation as with meticulous scheduling. Keeping motivated means keeping faith in your ability to see your tasks through.

For instance, let's see how a manager at a public relations company makes effective use of her daily to-do list.

First, she notes from her schedule that she has an hour set aside for paperwork. For her to-do list, she looks at each sub-task in this hour and determines that preparing a client contract is time sensitive and high value. So she adds this to the list. This is an example of breaking items down.

Then she reviews her tasks to ensure they're worded in an objective and achievable manner. She considers the list item "Finish contract" and revises it to "Proof and approve contract by noon." Here she's creating realistic objectives.

Third, she checks her schedule for the next day and lists all the critical tasks. She then lists the high, medium, and low priority tasks. This is assigning priorities.

Next she compiles her list by adding her top ten most important tasks for the day. At 10:00 a.m., her boss calls to reschedule their weekly meeting to the next day. She reschedules the meeting and moves a lower priority item onto her task list to fill the spot. She's revising as needed.

Finally, she crosses each task off her list as she completes it. By the end of the day, she's completed every item on her list, and leaves the office earlier than her less-efficient colleagues. See how she's keeping herself motivated. Creating an effective to-do list is a necessary and important part of personal scheduling - but it's just as important to make effective use of that list. Following these core guidelines will keep you on track.

ACHIEVE PRODUCTIVITY IN YOUR PERSONAL LIFE

It's difficult to stay on top of a busy work schedule and at the same time balance family responsibilities, personal goals, and trips away. Achieving productivity in your personal life will help you keep a sensible balance between home and work.

In this book, you'll learn how to prepare for trips, plan personal and household tasks, and become more organized as a parent. You'll also explore tips for getting out the door in the morning and for maintaining your well-being.

1. Getting Out the Door
2. Staying Organized on the Go
3. Organizing Your Personal and Household Tasks
4. Becoming an Organized Parent in a Busy World
5. Keeping Health and Well-being on Your To-do List

GETTING OUT THE DOOR

After completing this topic, you should be able to identify tips to help you to get yourself and your family out the door on time.

You wake up in the morning, get dressed, and have breakfast...it's almost time to leave for work. Sounds simple, right? The kids are up and ready...you're about to leave. Then it hits you. The school lunches...the dirty laundry...the empty gas tank! The list of things to do feels endless and you think to yourself "I'll never get out the door!"

Everyone has had a morning like this at some point. For many, this is the most hectic part of the day, and is filled with last minute chores and frantic activity. But it doesn't have to be this way. By using a few simple tips, you can turn getting out the door in the morning into a stress-free routine.

The first tip is to prepare ahead. The night before, pick out your and the children's clothes – making sure they're pressed and clean. Make and pack the lunch, get the table ready for breakfast, and leave out nonperishable foods like cereals, so they're ready to be grabbed first thing in the morning.

Before they go to bed, have children pack their schoolbags with their homework, textbooks, permission slips or gym clothes. Don't forget to pack your own briefcase or laptop bag with any devices or paperwork you'll need that day.

It's also a good idea to fill up your gas tank the day before, so you'll have enough for the morning. For instance, you could make it a habit to fill up during your lunch break, or on the way back home from work. And of book, don't misplace your car keys – you won't get far without them! Always leave them in the same place – such as on a hook, or in a dish near the front door. You could even leave them on your lunchbox, so you don't forget either of them in the morning.

The next tip is to teach children to become responsible for getting themselves ready in the morning. Young children will always need your help for this, but by first grade, they should know what they need to do and how to do it. At the outset, create a checklist and help children make their beds and tidy their rooms. Eventually they should be able to complete these chores on their own so that they're ready to leave on time.

Next, time wasters – avoid them! If it's not related to getting out the door in the morning, then don't do it. So don't read e-mails, pay nonurgent bills, or put on laundry loads that can wait until later.

Finally, use a monthly planner. This is great for maintaining and updating a schedule and for figuring out who's responsible for certain weekly chores...like whose turn it is to take out the trash.

By using these few basic tips, you can avoid the morning mad dash and get out the door on time and stress free.

STAYING ORGANIZED ON THE GO

After completing this topic, you should be able to select tips that help you manage time when you're on the go.

Do you ever find traveling for vacation or business a chaotic experience? Do you worry that you'll lose track of important tasks...fall behind on your reading...or that you'll end up having to buy new clothing or toiletries while on the road? Just because you're on the go doesn't mean your personal organization plans are out the window. All it takes is a little organization and preparation before – and during – your trip to make sure it goes smoothly.

First of all, plan your to-do list. By spending twenty minutes at the end of each week and ten at the end of each day on your to-do list, you'll be better able to keep track of things while away. It also helps you remember the day's activities, allowing you to be more fully present if on vacation with your family.

You'll also often hear people complain about all the time they've wasted waiting...at airports, in doctors' offices, in traffic or for the bus. But life is full of delays, and you can easily use this downtime constructively by planning for and taking advantage of these quiet periods. For instance, instead of getting worked up over a delayed appointment, you could save articles on your smartphone to read later, or carry a light paperback book with you for "offline" reading.

Stuck in traffic? How about downloading some of your favorite podcasts and listening to them to pass the time productively?

You could also use these periods of downtime to catch up with friends, or to organize and update your to-do list. Of book, you should never allow yourself to be distracted while driving. So even if you're stuck in traffic, ensure you're obeying local laws with regard to what, if anything, you can do on your phone while you're behind the wheel.

A useful tip for frequent travelers is to keep toiletries and other similar items packed and ready. This saves you time and money each time you travel – and cuts down on all those half-used bottles of shampoo.

When you're on the go, make sure to leave plenty of buffer time between your various activities. You might have planned ahead, but there are always unexpected snags to delay things; give yourself an extra five to ten minutes per task to ensure you can wrap up one task in time to prepare for the next.

But what if you don't have a book to read, or a device to listen to? Why not just accept it and make time for stillness? It might sound counterintuitive, but taking the time to do nothing while on the go can really help you become more productive. Just five minutes of silence and stillness has benefits such as reducing anxiety, clearing thoughts, providing solutions to problems, and making your work more pleasurable.

So don't waste your time wasting time; plan ahead and make your downtime work for you.

ORGANIZING YOUR PERSONAL AND HOUSEHOLD TASKS

After completing this topic, you should be able to identify tips that aid you in organizing personal and household tasks.

Chores. They're a drudgery no one enjoys, but a necessity for maintaining a clean and tidy house. Without proper organization, these menial tasks can sometimes get out of hand...taking up time you would rather be doing something you enjoy. But there are some straightforward ways of overcoming these issues.

You could, for example, consider hiring someone to clean your house. Don't just dismiss this as a luxury for the wealthy. Think about all your household chores, and the amount of time you and your family spend on them over the book of a year. By hiring a cleaner, you could spare yourself entire days' worth of cleaning. They can also clean an entire house in about four hours for a rate that will probably cost less than what it would cost you in terms of your time and effort.

Another time-consuming chore is grocery shopping. Driving to and from the store...finding a parking space...waiting in line at the checkout – all of this can take hours. But with so many stores now offering online options, you can take the hassle out of shopping and simply use delivery services. And, factoring in the price of gas – and the value of your time – in many cases it works out much cheaper.

Besides shopping and household chores, many people complain about how difficult it is to keep track of personal and household tasks, and to remember birthdays and anniversaries. These problems can easily be solved by creating master to-do lists and birthday/anniversary lists.

When creating a master to-do list, quickly jot down all the must-do entries you can think of. Don't bother analyzing or organizing at this point. Just get them out of your head. Once you've noted everything, then create your daily to-do list.

Next, make a list of friends and family members whose birthday or anniversary you would like to buy a card for, noting the date of each. Using this list, buy all your cards at once. Mark the recipient's name and important date in the corner of the envelope, so the stamp will cover it when you send it. And organize the cards by month. You can also use this same list to write down any gift ideas.

So, by now you should have made enough time to finally catch up on your reading, right? But what if you still don't have time to read all your magazines cover to cover? If this seems unrealistic, use the following shortcuts to stay ahead of your magazine and online reading. For paper magazines, go through the table of contents and tear out only the articles that interest you making sure to recycle the rest of the magazine. Or, if you prefer to read articles online, download an app that lets you personalize articles by your interests.

Chores don't have to take up all of your valuable personal time – a little planning and assistance can make household tasks and catching up on your reading a breeze.

BECOMING AN ORGANIZED PARENT IN A BUSY WORLD

After completing this topic, you should be able to choose actions that help you to organize your parental responsibilities.

As a parent, you're constantly juggling obligations and chores – preparing food, doing school runs, managing the kids' schedule. These all need to be planned ahead. To help you become a more organized parent, there are a few key tips that you can try.

First, keep cooking simple...your house isn't a restaurant after all! Try to create a weekly menu that all the family will like and that is easy to prepare. Rotating meals on a weekly basis means you can, for the most part, plan your shopping list once and reuse it each week. You could also cook large batches at a time to freeze and reheat later in the week. But change things up every couple of months – your diet needs variety and excitement.

Sometimes as a parent, you'll also get requests to cook something for a special occasion, like a scout meeting or a birthday party. This can put pressure on you – especially if you've already a busy schedule. Be realistic about what you've got time for – you can't accommodate every request. So don't feel guilty about getting store-bought treats, or offering to pay for party items instead.

Next, think about exchanging your services with neighbors or other parents. If they hate a chore that you love, you could offer to trade chores. Say, you hate washing windows but love gardening. You could trade one chore for the other, and vice versa.

Alternatively, you could pay a high school or college student to carry out some basic chores. By having them do babysitting, mowing the lawn, or painting around the house, you're not only saving yourself time and effort, but also teaching them key life skills, such as taking responsibility.

And, of book, having a "Plan B" in case your best-laid plans go astray is vitally important. If a family member gets sick, you get a flat tire, or are stuck in a storm, having an arrangement in place with a neighbor, relative, or friend to help you out will give you some peace of mind.

Another tip is to avoid letting children overschedule themselves. Soccer practice, music lessons, dance classes – the list of after-school activities can seem endless, with each one requiring a pickup or drop-off. Instead, have your older kids pick their favorite activities and drop the rest. This leaves more time for assignments or family-based activities.

Finally, to manage you and your kids time better, curb time spent on computers, tablets, playing video games, or watching TV. Time wasted watching TV, or on Internet-enabled devices, could be better spent on family hobbies or outdoors activities.

This doesn't mean you need to stop using these devices altogether. For example, you could choose certain times of the day when children can play video games, or make a list of TV shows that they're allowed to watch. Applying these few steps can have an immeasurable – and positive – impact on both your workload and the quality of your family time.

KEEPING HEALTH AND WELL-BEING ON YOUR TO-DO LIST

After completing this topic, you should be able to identify actions that help you maintain your health and well-being.

Why is that so many people don't make looking after their health a priority? Ask around and you'll probably get the same answer: not enough time. When life gets busy, people tend to put healthy habits like exercising, eating healthy, and getting enough sleep on the back burner.

It might sound selfish, but every now and then you need to look after number one – you're no good to anyone if you're tired, cranky, or sick. So let's explore some tips that can help you keep your health and well-being a priority on your to- do list.

First, schedule some downtime for yourself. Don't feel guilty about taking time off to relax, turning down a nonurgent request, or pampering yourself occasionally. After all, everyone needs a little downtime to stay at their productive best.

In fact, taking an unscheduled vacation day can sometimes be the perfect remedy when you're starting to feel burned out. Think of it as a form of therapy – it helps you to relax, refreshes you, and makes you more focused.

Next, get enough sleep. It can't be overstated how important a proper night's sleep is to your overall health and well-being. Poor sleep weakens your immune system, increasing your risk of infection and illness. It also decreases productivity and quality of work. Think about it – if you can barely keep your eyes open, errors are bound to creep in. This is because poor sleep impairs your concentration, memory, and judgment.

So make sure you develop a bedtime routine. For example, switch off electronic devices an hour before going to sleep, cut down on coffee, do some reading, meditate, and set yourself a regular sleep schedule.

Something else that can help you with your sleep – and your health – is getting enough exercise. Exercise is the number one factor influencing our well-being, and yet so few people do it on a regular basis. Common excuses are work or family commitments, but it only takes five to ten minutes of intense exercise for you to notice improvements in your physical and mental health.

One final tip to keep health on your to-do list is to use your time wisely. It's easy to get stuck doing nonurgent tasks when you could be doing something better with your time. Be selective! Before launching into a task, ask yourself "Do I really need to do this right now?" With so many demands on your free time, you need to choose the ones that provide some health benefits.

You might also consider asking for a flexible work schedule – this will give you extra time when you need it. For instance, if you worked a compressed workweek of, say, four 10-hour days, this would give an extra day for appointments or simply relaxation. Or, you could get to work early – or work through lunch – to give you extra time in the afternoon to get to the gym.

So no more excuses. Develop a wellness plan, make your health your priority, and stick to it!

www.ingramcontent.com/pod-product-compliance
Lightning Source LLC
Chambersburg PA
CBHW071110220526
45467CB00004B/1784

9798687547604